D1127624

Pepper in My Pancakes

BY CHLOE HOWARD

Published by The Writer's Boutique

One beautiful day,

while Daddy was away,

Mama and I went singing and

dancing into the kitchen,

bright and early,

still wearing our PJs

with plans to make my favorite...

the **yummiest** of yums,

PANCAKES!

I just love **pancakes**.

I especially like mine with **extra fluff** and topped with butter and hot syrup.

Mama prefers hers with whipped cream, **sugared strawberries**, and a side of hot tea.

But, no matter what the topping or side, the magic is always in the recipe.

So, we started our pancakes with a big bowl,
mixing in ingredients like:

FLOUR, BAKING POWDER, SUGAR, BAKING SODA,
SALT, EGG, VANILLA, and BUTTERMILK.

Then we used a long wooden spoon to

stir

  and **stir**

    and **stir**

      until the batter was slightly lumpy.

After stirring, we turned the timer on for
23 minutes to let the batter rest. This makes the
pancakes just right and fluffy how I like them.

It also gave Mama and I enough time
to clean up and get dressed.

Now, it just so happens that on this most **beautifulest** day, Mr. Pepper, the sly ole neighborhood fox, was creeping about trying to ruin anybody's day or dish with his infamous pepper.

So, of course, Mr. Pepper somehow snuck in through our back door, while no one was in the kitchen, and...

He went right to work
        on ruining our pancakes
                with sprinkles of his

BLACK PEPPER.

Just as he was going in for his final shake,
we **caught** him in the act and Mama said,

"**Why** in the **world**
would you put **PEPPER**
in our **pancakes** you
silly fox?"

Then we both **sneezed** so loudly that
Mr. Pepper jumped and hit the ceiling.

Mama grabbed the broom and that fox went

ZOOM

...right out of the house.

Leaving us with a mess of pepper in our pancakes to deal with.

I was near tears,
but the damage was already done.

Mama **hugged** me tight and
told me she just might have a fix.

AND FIX IT, SHE DID!

With a little **love** and a few more ingredients:

GINGER

LEMON JUICE

CINNAMON

NUTMEG

and a **big** spoon of

BROWN SUGAR

She gave that batter another good stir, heated the skillet with a dab of oil, then started flipping those pancakes and stacking them high.

When we finished,
   I got to be the first taster,
   and to my

surprise...

those
pancakes
were
DELISH!!!

WHO KNEW?

That ole fox thought he could ruin our recipe with his **PEPPER**. But with a bit of love and a few yummy ingredient changes, we overcame that peppery obstacle.

I learned that day:

NEVER ALLOW A LITTLE PEPPER TO KEEP ME FROM MY

PANCAKES!

Mama ate hers with **whipped cream**,
sugared strawberries, and a side of hot tea.

Me? Well, I especially loved mine with
butter, **hot syrup**, and that good 'o fluff.

In the end, it really was the most **beautiful**
day indeed!

THE END

The Recipe
Pepper In My Pancakes

What you will Need

- Large Mixing Bowl
- Small Mixing Bowl
- Wooden Spoon
- Whisk
- Measuring Cups
- Measuring Spoons
- Pan or Griddle
- Apron (Us fashion chefs wear aprons to keep the mess off our dress ...)
- An adult when cooking over a hot stove

Ingredients

- 1 1/4 cup flour
- 2T Sugar
- 2t Baking powder
- 1/2t Baking soda
- 1/2t Kosher salt
- 1T Vanilla
- 1 egg
- 1c buttermilk **
- 1/4t ground black pepper
- 1T brown sugar
- 1/2t cinnamon
- 1/8t ginger
- a pinch of nutmeg
- 1t lemon juice
- 1T melted butter
- Olive oil as needed to lightly grease skillet
- Toppings

Directions

Step ① - Combine flour, sugar, baking powder, baking soda, and salt into a large bowl.

Step ② - In a separate small bowl whisk together the egg, milk, and vanilla. Gradually pour liquid into the flour bowl and mix with wooden spoon until well moistened and slightly lumpy.

Step ③ - Let the batter rest for 20 minutes at room temperature before continuing.

Step ④ - Add pepper, cinnamon, ginger, brown sugar, nutmeg, and melted butter (hint: make sure butter is not hot and stir a little after each ingredient is added). Let batter rest again for another 3-5 min.

Step ⑤ - Pre-heat griddle on medium heat and add a small bit of oil, just enough to slightly grease and lightly fry the pancake.

Step ⑥ - Pour batter onto the skillet (make your pancakes as big or small as you'd like). Cook until bubbles form and the edges look dry (about 3 to 4 minutes). Flip and cook until browned on the other side about another 3 to 4 minutes more. Remove from heat and butter. Repeat with remainining batter, adding additional oil to the pan as needed.

Step ⑦ - Top as you so desire. Some tasty topping ideas include HOT syrop, butter, whip cream, sugared strawberries, and/or pecans.

** If you don't have buttermilk, you can always create your own souring concoction by adding 1.5 T (15 ml) vinegar or lemon juice to 1 cup of milk. Allow it to sit and sour for 5 minutes before using.

Feeds 4-5 People

And, don't forget to say grace

Final Word...

Be on guard for those foxes, the mischievous little foxes that are always on the hunt and would love nothing more than to steal your joy and ruin the day. If ever such a fox douses your recipe, remember there are ingredients that can overcome the power of pepper:

PATIENCE + LOVE + POSITIVITY + FORGIVENESS + HOPE

xoxo, Mom

(Inspired by Song of Solomon 2:15)

Dedicated to the GOD,
who works all things together for the good of those who love Him!
(Roman 8:28)

Special Thanks & Credits:

Thank you Dad, Mom, Grandma Phyllis, Grandma Emma, God-mommy Michelle, Anastasia, Audy Popoola, and all of our family and friends for your continuous prayers and support. Love, Chloe

My sweet daughter, keep writing and reaching for new galaxies! You are SO loved... Mom

Pepper In My Pancakes
2011, 2016, 2020 Chloe Howard & Nichole Howard

Illustrations hand drawn by Anastasia Azhimova for The Writer's Boutique.

Please share pictures of your pancake creations with us on social media using hashtag: #PepperInMyPancakes.

The Writer's Boutique
a creative + publishing company
PO Box 901329
Kansas City, MO 64190

Library of Congress Number: 2020901433
ISBN: 978-1-7345574-0-4

www.thewritersboutique.com

Chloe + Chole

MADE IN KANSAS CITY USA

THE
Writer's
BOUTIQUE
CO.

Hello Friends!

We'd like to take this opportunity to shine a spotlight on the women of **TIMBALI CRAFTS** who help to feed more than 3,000 orphans and vulnerable children each day in rural Eswatini. The nearly 100 Timbali women, from more than 20 communities, serve as volunteer cooks at community 'Care Points', helping to meet a tremendous need!

Timbali means 'flowers' in Saswatti, the Swazi language. It's also used to translate 'lilies' in Matthew, chapter 6, where Jesus talks about how God's generous provision for the 'lilies of the field' pales in comparison to His provision for His children; and that we don't have to worry, because He knows our needs and He can meet those needs better than we ever could ourselves.

In a similar spirit, **TIMBALI CRAFTS** helps to provide not only an income for these incredibly hardworking women, but opportunities for empowerment, friendship, and spiritual growth.

So, please go online today and visit timbalicrafts.org to learn more. **TIMBALI CRAFTS** is a ministry of Pour International, a U.S. 501c3 organization. Your prayers and purchases become a partnership that helps to deliver hope and support in a tangible way for this amazing cause.

Chloe + Chole

Beautiful Products. Inspiring Women. Handmade in Eswatini, Africa.

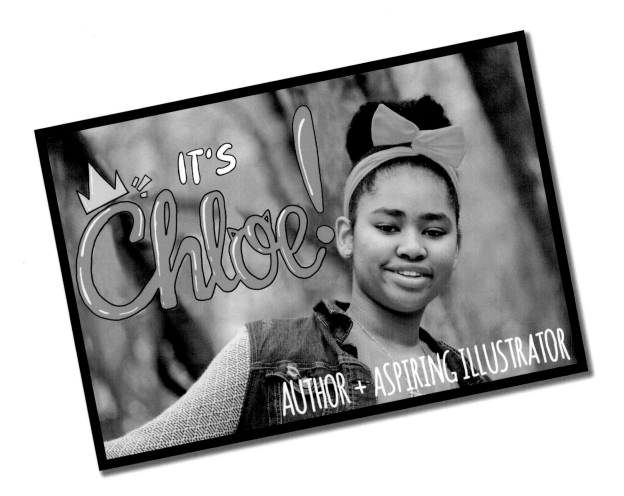

Thanks, Ms. Hadtis

— Chloe Howard